Amit Grinfeld

IRANIAN FOREIGN POLICY
FROM AN ISRAELI POINT OF VIEW

Translation: Blue Lion Language Services

Cover and Book design: Studio Lev Ari

Amit Grinfeld

Iranian foreign policy from an Israeli point of view

···◆···

"We only see what we know"

Johann Wolfgang von Goethe

Table of Contents

The Azadi Tower in Tehran.

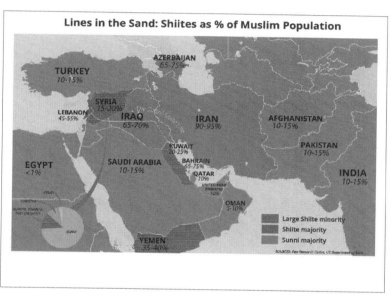

Map taken from the Times of Israel (Credit: Pew Research)

A perspective of Iran in view of the United States' withdrawn from the nuclear agreement

The Islamic Republic of Iran has gained considerable attention in the headlines of the global media. Most articles on Iran deal with its various struggles: its struggle against U.S. sanctions, its struggle against the Sunni world headed by Saudi Arabia, its struggle against Israel, its struggle against the rebels in Syria, its struggle against domestic opposition and much more besides. This article reviews Iranian foreign policy and the assertive, intensive international activity that the Islamic Republic has been advancing and attempts to explain them. The maps and photographs in this article have taken from the free database of the Internet encyclopedia (Wikipedia).

A few general words about Iran

Iran is a very large country, and with an area of 636 thousand square miles, is but slightly smaller than Alaska. It is located at the eastern edge of the Middle East and has borders with seven countries: Iraq, Turkey, Armenia, Azerbaijan, Turkmenistan, Pakistan and Afghanistan. Iran has a coast on the Caspian Sea, the Persian Gulf and the Gulf of Oman. Most of Iran's area is desert and desolate, but it has a few mountain ranges, large lakes, rivers and many fertile areas. Iran's population is very large, at approximately 82 million people, more than half of whom are under the age of 30. Most Iranians belong to the Persian ethnic group, which has an ancient, splendid history including a number of enormous empires. Alongside the persons, most of whom follow Shia Islam, there are diverse other groups living in Iran. Iran has ethnic minorities that include Azeris, Kurds, Arabs, Afghans, Jews and others. In addition there is religious diversity between the Shiite majority and minorities such as Sunni Muslims, Christians, Jews, Bahais and Zoroasters. The Zoroasters have been maintaining Persia's ancient religion despite 14 centuries of Muslim dominance.

Iran's enormous area is very rich in natural resources and contains some of the largest gas and oil fields in the world. Almost 10% of global oil reserves and approximately 15% of global natural gas reserves known today are in Iran. Therefore it is unsurprising that Iran's economy is strongly based on oil and gas exports and about 60% of its revenues come from this sector. The Iranian Administration invests considerably in attempts to diversify the Iranian economy and making it more diverse and modern, with only partial success. The Iranian investment in human capital, particularly in higher education institutes, is very extensive. Hundreds of thousands of young Iranians graduate from higher education each year.

Modern Iran

Modern Iran's borders were sharped in the Teheran Conference of 1943. Once World War Two ended, Iran became an independent country. The forces of the allies and Soviets that had camped in it pulled out. A decade and a half of unstable democratic administration in Iran ended in a military coup in 1953. With the help of the U.S. CIA and Britain's MI6, the "Shah", the Iranian king who led a pro-western dictatorship in Iran was reinstated. For the next 26 years, the Iranian dynasty of kings advanced its country deep into the modern world and Iran transformed from being an agrarian country to a strong, industrialized one and exporter of oil and gas. Iran's army procured many western combat platforms such as American F-14 Tomcat fighters, which were considered an advanced jet in the 1970s. Iran enjoyed great investment from foreign companies, including Israeli ones, in its economy and infrastructures. At the same time, the Shah's regime was extremely corrupt. Many simple Iranians did not gain any economic prosperity while the Shah and his cronies became rich. Finally, after years of increasing unrest, the conditions in Iran were ripe for revolution. The masses poured into the streets and collapsed the government and the Iranian Shah fled the country.

The end of the Shah regime period: soldiers aiming their rifles at demonstrators. Iran, 1978.

The Iranians who called for change in the streets welcomed the rise of a new regime, which completely differed from its predecessor. In 1979, Iran became an extremist Shiite Islam theocracy. This Islamic revolution was led by Ayatollah (a senior Shiite religious leader) Khomeini, who was in exile in Paris at that time. Khomeini was flown to Iran by the French, who hoped that his great popularity in Iran would lead to stability in the country and a repeat of its pro-western policy. They were wrong. Iran's foreign policy became very hostile towards the west, hostile to dictatorship regimes of Arab countries and hostile even to Soviet Russia. From a state of an economy that was attractive to foreign investments, Iran became an isolated, sharia Muslim state. The national laws were rewritten, this time under strict Muslim influence, immediately leading to many changes. For example, in today's Iran, a woman walking in the street with her head uncovered is breaking the law. Another example: homosexuality in Iran is a capital offense. More than a thousand people are executed in Iran each year, mostly owing to offenses attributed to offending Islam. The constitution of the Iranian Islamic Republic calls for elections every 4 years. Elections in Iran are not really free, because all candidates for election to the parliament and presidency are first approved by the supreme leader. The first supreme leader of the Islamic Republic was, as stated, Khomeini. Today it is Ayatollah Ali Khamenei, who took power upon Khomeini's death.

After the revolution, a new political military arm was established in Iran, which exists alongside the army: the Revolutionary Guards. This is a security agency that is intended to protect the Iranian regime against enemies foreign and domestic. Some of the Revolutionary Guard units are open and official, whereas others operate as a secret police of terrorism and fear. Along with the Revolutionary Guards, another military force was established, the Al Quds Force. The Al Quds Force answers to the Revolutionary Guards and serves as an arm for advancing the Islamic revolution outside of Iran. The regime in Iran has two primary ideological goals: the first is maintaining the revolutionary regime in Iran and the second is advancing and exporting the Islamic revolution and its values, firstly across the Shiite region and later worldwide.

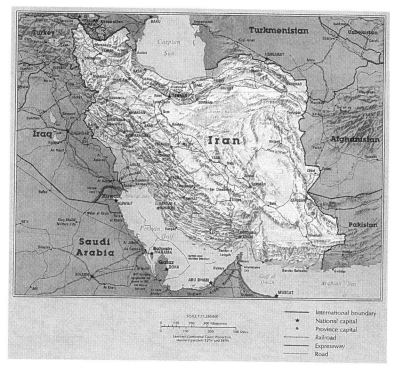

A map of Iran

The wars of the 1980s

I n the years after the Islamic revolution, two terrible wars commenced in Iran, on either side of the country: in Afghanistan, Islamic rebels started to fight the pro-Soviet regime in 1979 and later fought the Soviets (the Afghanistan War). In effect, Afghanistan has been torn by wars ever since. Iran distanced itself from direct involvement of its military in Afghanistan, but its intelligence agencies support some of the militias fighting there, primarily the Shiite ones. Many Afghan refugees fled to Iran. Out of the resulting chaos, drug dealers and traffickers started to cross the border between the two countries with ease.

On the other side, on Iran's western border, a lethal, long war started against Iraq. The Iraqi tyrant Saddam Hussein, was furious over the support that revolutionary Iran gave to Kurdish rebels in his country. He invaded western Iran in 1980 hoping to strike it and annex areas containing Arab populations and large amounts of oil. Hussein attacked Iran, which had three times his own country's size and population, because he believed that the revolution had weakened it. Iraq deployed a large army with the latest Soviet weaponry. That army sometimes used chemical weapons.

During the fighting, the construction of an Iraqi nuclear reactor was completed, the aim of which was developing atomic weapons. The Iranian Airforce, which had weakened in the absence of U.S. support (mainly due to a shortage of spare parts) was unable to incapacitate the reactor. But in 1981 an Israeli Air Force raid destroyed it completely. Israel not only saved itself from an existential threat but also indirectly assisted the Iranians, denying the Iraqi tyrant a doomsday weapon.

The Iran-Iraq war lasted until 1988. Revolutionary Iran demonstrated impressive tenacity. The leader, Khomeini, and his advisors, did not hesitate to sacrifice many solders to compensate for their inferiority in arms. Tens of thousands of teenagers and children were pressed into military services. In many battles, Iranian children were sent to run into Iraqi minefields to clear paths in them by detonating them with their bodies. These children had small plastic keys tied around their necks to symbolize the keys to heaven, where they would arrive owing to their sacrifice. After vicious battles, the Iraqi invader was repelled and chased back into his own country.

An Iranian boy solider during the Iran-Iraq War

After 8 years, the Iran-Iraq war ended. Iran sustained about 600,000 deaths and nearly a quarter of a trillion dollars' worth of economic damage. Iran and Iraq's borders were unchanged. Iran turned to like its wounds and Saddam Hussein's Iraq quickly invaded its small, oil rich neighbor Kuwait. This was an aggressive move that led to Iraq's defeat in the Gulf War. The United States, which led the international coalition against Iraq, did not lead the armies to the point of Saddam Hussein's ouster. He was left in power, under restrictions, for several reasons, two of which were: as a violent dictator, Hussein could keep Iraq united under an iron fist, and secondly, Hussein was an adversary of Iran and as long as he controlled Iraq, the Islamic Revolution could not encroach on his country or spread beyond it.

The Iranians looked at Saddam Hussein's antics in the 1980s and early 2000s and learned a number of lessons. Tehran decided not to waive the wish to export the Islamic revolution, but its aggressive foreign policy was refined and polished. Exporting the revolution became quieter and more covert. Post-1989 Iran has always preferred to employ proxy organizations and allies rather than operating directly. Above all, Iran decided that it must obtain the best insurance certificate of all: nuclear weapons.

Revolutionary Iran starts to develop a nuclear program

In 1989, supreme leader Khomeini died. Ali Khamenei took his place. Khamenei is considered an extremist conservative, even in the terms of Iran's Islamic revolution. He never leaves Iran. Khamenei often clashes with moderate factions in Iran's parliament and constantly tries to restrict their power. Because he considers Israel and the United States to be bitter adversaries, they are referred in Iran of his times as "the great Satan" and "the small Satan". He does not support any kind of dialog with or recognition of Israel and openly calls for its destruction. Khamenei also outspokenly opposes any negotiations with the USA. According to the Reuters news agency, Khamenei has assets worth 95 billion dollars.

Left: supreme leader Khomeini (1979-1989). Right: supreme leader Khamenei (1989-today)

Khamenei rekindled Iran's nuclear program, which had been frozen by its predecessor Khomeini, who considered nuclear weapons to be un-Islamic. In effect, the roots of the development of Iran's nuclear program started back in the 1960s when the west asked to build nuclear reactors there for electricity. Officially, Iran argues that its nuclear plan is intended for peaceful purposes, i.e. generating electricity, medicine, research and development. However, according to intelligence reports of western countries and the International Atomic Energy Agency, this is a lie: Iran's nuclear program is intended above all for developing nuclear weapons. In May 2018, Israel showed a complete Iranian archive that had been stolen by the Mossad, its central intelligence organization. The archive was filled with clear proof that Iran was working on developing nuclear bombs and missiles capable of carrying them.

Unlike Iraq, the Iranians decided to advance their nuclear power gradually and in a decentralized manner. Saddam Hussein concentrated all of his effort in building a single primary reactor. That reactor depended completely on the import of raw materials and radioactive fuels. Therefore, when Israel destroyed the reactor, Iraq's nuclear program was effectively destroyed. Iraq of the 1980s did not have the money or know-how to restart the program. Contemporary Iran is a completely different story. It has the money, particularly given the fact that its military programs are budgeted before everything else. It has the motivation, and just as importantly, the know-how. The scientists and engineers in Iran's nuclear project are mostly Iranians (with North Koran, Russian and other assistance). There is no doubt that the Iranians are gradually acquiring extensive knowledge in the field and are learning from experience while making headway. This is all being done under the pretext of development of a civilian nuclear program, which is not prohibited under international law.

As a tactical lesson from the destruction of the Iraqi reactor, Iran decided to spread its nuclear facilities far from each other over its large territory. Instead of one reactor, Iran is building multiple reactors and facilities for enriching uranium using various methods. There are a number of uranium farms in the country and enrichment of uranium mined in Iran is done primarily using specialized centrifuges. By doing so, Iran is gradually ensuring independent nuclear ability, while minimizing its dependence on import of raw materials. Most of its nuclear facilities, and certainly it military ones, are dug under many meters of concrete and rock and are carefully defended. An airstrike against Iran's nuclear program is possible, but would be very complicated and would not be likely to destroy all installations. Even if all installations are destroyed, Iran is capable of quickly rebuilding them.

Iran has been investing great resources in developing know-how and indigenous production capabilities in the ballistic missiles filed. Some if this capability already allows Iran to launch satellites of its manufacture into space. At the same time it currently possesses hundreds of missiles of various types, some of which are capable of reaching as far as Eastern Europe. Iranian scientists are currently developing even longer ranged missiles, which may strike at Central and even Western Europe. They are also working on warheads that convertible for use in carrying nuclear weapons. This fact was clearly revealed upon the publication of Iranian archive that the Israeli Mossad obtained. Iran's ambition is being capable of launching nuclear missiles at targets thousands of miles away.

Why is the Iranian regime aiming to achieve nuclear weapons? There are a number of reasons for this:

1. Nuclear weapons represent "insurance" against attacks from overseas. Even the strongest countries are hesitant in attacking a regime that is in possession of multiple nuclear bombs.

2. Under nuclear protection, Iran will be able to handle its armed proxy organizations more aggressively, without being too fearful of retribution actions aimed directly against it. A nuclear Iran will be able to establish hegemony in the Middle East more easily and become a regional power and even a global one.

3. Nuclear weapons give their holders prestige. There are few countries in the world with such weapons (only

11 in effect, and some add Israel to the list). This is military capability that transmits power. This power can deter not only foreign enemies but also domestic opposition organizations. The Iranian people, the regime hopes, will unite around the leadership if it successfully achieves the weapon.

An antiaircraft gun defending the nuclear facility at Natanz

The first decade of the 2000s – America fights on either side of Iran

The 9/11 attacks led the USA to decide to invade Afghanistan back in late 2001. Since then, U.S. forces and their allies have been fighting the Taliban and other terrorist organizations in a desultory manner. In 2003, the USA also invaded Iraq, deposing Saddam Hussein and his regime. Iraq collapsed and was engulfed in chaos. Armed militias, most of which has an extremist Islamic ideology, started to fight the Americans. Iran's traditional enemy was wiped out, courtesy of the United States. At that stage, Iran was left relatively restrained, as giant forces of the USA and its allies were fighting terrorism both on its eastern border (Afghanistan) and its western one (Iraq). These wars led to new influxes of refugees into Iran. Today there are about 2.5 million refugees in Iran, many of whom are Shiites who have fled from Afghanistan.

American tanks in Baghdad, 2003

The sanctions on Iran, the collapse of its economy and the fury of the Iranian people

Since Khomeini's rise to power in 1979, Iran has been subjected to the pressure of sanctions at various levels from the United States. Once the telltale signs of Iran's attempts to build nuclear weapons started to appear, the United States started to apply increasingly strict sanctions against it. The USA was able to harness the Europeans in the move, and even the Russians and Chinese cooperated to a reasonable degree. The Iranian regime tried to contend with the economic isolation through a range of means: trading on the black market, using strawman companies, smuggling, deals with criminal organizations, various brokers and other methods. But this was only partially successful. Iran's economy was severely damaged following the sanctions and its international image deteriorated further. The Iranian currency, the riyal, lost a lot of its value. Exports and imports from and to the country were restricted, the prices of products in Iran's streets rose and many educated young people found themselves unable to find work or a future in their country. Bitterness and fury started to engulf Iran's streets.

In 2009, presidential elections were held in Iran. The Iranian people, it is estimated, voted for a presidential candidate who was considered to be moderate. It must be remembered that even that candidate, Hassan Musawi, was cleared to contend by the administration before the elections. However, the elections were clearly falsified and the extremist conservative president Mahmoud Ahmadinejad was reelected after having received 67% of the votes. The masses swept into the streets to demonstrate, demanding a reform and change of power in favor of a government that cared for its citizens. The police and armed militias headed by the Basij, violent bullies in the employ of the regime – quelled the riots forcefully. Hundreds were killed and thousands injured, and thousands more were arrested and imprisoned under poor conditions. Some of the detainees "disappeared". The leaders of the west, headed by Barack Obama, the President of the United States, chose not to intervene. The regime survived owing to its great violence against its people and the fact that no foreign aid or abetting arrived. However, since 2009 it has been clear that the revolutionary ayatollahs regime has strong resistance, which is currently being oppressed. Demonstrations still occur from time to time, and there are even strikes, which are prohibited under Iranian law.

A burning bus in the middle of a street during the demonstrations in Iran in 2009.

The Arab Spring as an opportunity for exporting the Islamic revolution

The Arab world, consisting of various dictatorships, has undergone a list of changes in the last decade, accompanied by social, political and economic tremors. The all too generic name given to this broad phenomenon is the Arab Spring. Since 2011, Arab regimes have been overthrown by the pressure of giant demonstrations of frustrated masses in the streets. This article does not deal directly with the Arab Spring, but for covering Iran, a few words should be written about what happened in the following countries:

Tunisia in North Africa was the first country to burn with mass demonstrations. The president fled by the skin of his teeth and after a period of shocks a new government was established with partial stability.

In Libya, the situation quickly deteriorated into a civil war. The veteran, cruel and bizarre tyrant Muamar Gadhafi was killed by rebels who received extensive assistance from NATO's air forces. Since then Libya has remained chaotic and violent.

In Egypt, which is the most populous Arab country, Hosni Mubarak's regime collapsed. President Mubarak was a long-standing ally of the USA. The U.S. President Obama decided not to support Mubarak but instead preferred to support free elections in Egypt. Mubarak was quickly ousted and free elections were held. The Muslim Brotherhood won and gained control. Within two years they managed to crush the economy of the state, which was already poor, and its prosperous tourism vanished. General Muhamad A-Sisi led another revolution in 2013 and the Egyptian Army regained power and outlawed the Muslim Brotherhood.

Yemen: in early 2012, the government of the President of Yemen, who had been the local tyrant for twenty years, collapsed. The relative stability of this very poor country vanished and different forces, some of which were Islamic extremists, started to fight each other. A very active branch of Al Qaeda, an extremist Sunni organization, is flourishing in Yemen. At the same time, Houthi rebels, a Shiite organization, took over part of the country.

Syria: mass demonstrations against the Syrian tyrant Bashar al Assad broke out throughout the country in 2011. Bloody attempts to suppress them were unsuccessful and the demonstrations became a terrible civil war. After the west, headed by Barack Obama, decided again not to intervene, the rebel forces were unable to obtain arms and unite. The rebels splintered into innumerable armed militias, and strong jihadist forces started to set the tone. The rebels have been fighting the regime and each other ever since. The terrorist organization ISIS was able to establish an extremist Sunni Islam "state" in extensive territories of Syria and Iraq for some time under the cover of the chaos of the war. The regime, with the assistance of its allies – Russia and Iran, has been able to survive. Bashar al Assad has gradually been regaining control over the country. At the time of writing, the fighting is far from over. After more than seven years of war, Syria is almost completely devastated with at least half a million dead, five million refugees who have fled the country and 11 million internally displaced within Syria. Only a quarter of the Syrian population has not fled from its homes to date.

Iraq: After the U.S. army, with many casualties, was able to provide Iraq a certain degree of stability, President Obama decided to pull most troops out of the country in 2011. Within three years Iraq collapsed into its constituents – Shiites, Kurds and Sunnis. The ISIS terrorist organization was able in 2014-2017 to take over extensive territory in Iraq. It took the Government of Iraq and the Kurds three years to regain what ISIS conquered in a few weeks. ISIS brought to the chaos that started with the U.S. invasion in 2003 to its peak. This was a big opportunity for Iran to increase its fostering of strong Shiite militias in Iraq. There have been Iranian attempts in recent years to turn Iraq into a protégée country with the help of its Shiite majority. The last elections ,which were held in May 2018, showed that the Iraqis, including the Shiites among them, were unenthusiastic about accepting Iran's authority, but this does not mean that the struggles are over.

This caricature by artist Sherif Arafa describes Toppling the Arabic Totum – the overthrow of regimes in the Arab World

Agreements between the powers and Iran

The international sanctions against Iran proved effective over time and the Iranian regime is beginning to feel that it is being economically stifled. The 2009 riots have not been forgotten and the Ayatollahs are very familiar with the potential fury of their people. After the Iranian regime understood that it was on the brink of total economic collapse, it decided that it was time to compromise. After long negotiations, in 2013 the Iranians signed with the powers (the USA, Russia, China, France, Germany and Britain) an interim agreement. This interim agreement, called the Geneva interim agreement, acted to restrict Iran's nuclear program in exchange for partial removal of sanctions. The UN's atomic energy agency confirmed that Iran had gotten rid of most of the enriched Iranian already in its possession in exchange for the agreement. A similar additional interim agreement was signed in April 205 and is called the Lausanne agreement.

In July 2015, the negotiations matured into a permanent agreement between Iran and the powers, despite considerable resistance from both the USA (most of the U.S. Senate was against the agreement) and from Israel. It is interesting that there are also conservative extremists within Iran itself who are opposed to the agreement. This is opposition on an ideological basis that considers any negotiation and concession to be an act of submission and diminished honor.

Equal sized flags. The U.S. Secretary of State John Kerry and his team members in a meeting with Iran's foreign minister, Mohammad Zarif and his staff in 2016.

The essence of the agreement: Iran is to freeze its nuclear program and handover almost all uranium already enriched beyond basic enrichment. In exchange, the sanctions against it to be gradually removed and it subjects most of its facilities to UN inspection.

The supporters of the agreement argue that it is freezing Iran's nuclear program for at least fifteen years and provides a basis for dialog, mutual trade and peace and stability in the Middle East. According to the UN's atomic energy agency, Iran is honoring the terms of the agreement and western intelligence agencies confirm this.

The opponents of the agreement point out the following facts: the agreement restricts Iran only temporarily. Even if the program is suspended for now, Iran does not lose its development ability to achieve nuclear weapons in the long term. There are too few UN inspectors and their ability to reach nuclear sites is limited. Also, they must give the Iranians 24 hours warning before visiting sensitive sites. This is not true inspection. According to the agreement's opponents, Iran is gaining the removal of the sanctions against it while maintaining its nuclear development ability. Once Iran wishes to break the agreement or once it expires without a new valid being in place, it will be able to break forward within a short period to complete building nuclear weapons.

The agreement does not restrict Iran in the development (which is incessantly continuing) of ballistic missiles – the main launch platform of nuclear weapons. There is no mention of Iran's subversive, aggressive activity in various countries. Such activity has been continuing with greater zeal since the sanctions have been removed. In addition the agreement is subject to moral criticism – an agreement with a fundamentalist, unreliable regime that has lied throughout its history (and if anyone doubts this, the Israeli Mossad has provided the most recent proof of this). This is a regime that tramples human rights, violates the sovereignty of many countries, is calling for the destruction of Israel, a UN member state, and is jeers western values as a whole.

Almost immediately after the agreement, the USA under President Obama released large amounts of money that had been frozen to Iran. The extent of the amounts is debated – some argue that it is just hundreds of millions, whereas others state the figure to be 5-10 billion dollars while others say it is up to 150 billion dollars. Many companies, primarily European ones, started to sign giant investment and development contracts with Iran. While it will take years to understand how much money Iran has earned to date from the nuclear agreement, at the symbolic level and as contracts signed on paper, the Iranian economy has regained its growth potential. The Ayatollah regime has successfully showed the masses suffering in the streets an agreement that gives them hope, and reduces the chance of a popular uprising. It is important to note that Iran, at least potentially, is a key trade partner of countries such as Germany, Italy and

France. An increase in oil prices in the first half of 2018 and an increase in Iran's oil and gas exports also help its economy.

Despite all this, the situation of the average Iranian citizen is still far from improving. A series of earthquakes and severe droughts have been compounding the suffering in the lives of many in Iran. And where is the money that is coming in? In the three years since the nuclear agreement with Iran, its defense budget has increased by 40%. In addition, many rumors of corruption in the ayatollah regime indicate that a lot of money has simply been stolen. It is difficult to prove this in the absence of a fair legal and judicial system in Iran. It is interesting that Iran is allocating increasing diverse at the expense of its military to Revolutionary Guard forces. Particular, the budget of the Al Quds Force, which as mentioned is entrusted with advancing Iran's interests worldwide, has increased. In other words, there is less money for tanks and warplanes for the regular army and more money for advancing armed proxy organizations. This method suits the Iranian regime. It is a regime that always prefers to let protégé organizations operate on its behalf instead of overtly sending its forces to operate in other countries.

Today, Iran operates in the following countries:

Afghanistan: Iran's faltering neighbor shares a border that is nearly 600 miles with it. The two countries have ancient commercial and cultural ties. Since the U.S. invasion of Afghanistan, Iran has been involved in providing aid to gunmen fighting the U.S. military and the local government. Some of the jihadists fighting in Afghanistan have also been trained in camps in Iranian territory in recent years. Iran's involvement is limited in this country and its aim is probably to maintain a relatively low but constant level of violence, so that Afghanistan will not completely disintegrate, but the U.S. army will continue to bleed in its mountains. At the same time, Iran has an interest in stabilizing Afghanistan (without the Americans of course) in order to cut off the influx of refugees from it and the drug shipments that are entering Iran from its eastern neighbor.

Iraq: the destruction of the Saddam Hussein regime and incessant infighting in Iraq have become a rare opportunity for the Iranians to act. The Iranians have established in the Shiite parts of Iraq militias whose great power has assisted the weak Iraqi Army to repel ISIS. After the elimination of ISIS presence in Iraq, these militias do not seem to be on the brink of dissolution. At the same time, Iran is trying to take over Iraqi politics, based on the Shiite majority in the country. There is also an attempt to subject parts of Iraq's economy to Iranian companies in the guise of trade. Like in Lebanon, which we shall discuss shortly, the Iranians have established a militia called Hezbollah (God's party) in Iraq too.

Lebanon: the Shiite minority in the country has expanded in recent decades at a staggering pace because of its high birth rate. Today the Shiites are the largest group among Lebanon's citizens. For years, Iran has been supporting the well-armed Hezbollah Lebanese terrorist organization. The Hezbollah is the leading power in Lebanon today and has tens of thousands of fighters armed with modern weaponry. In the Lebanese political scene, in May 2018 the Hezbollah led a winning coalition in the country's elections. The Hezbollah is not only taking over Lebanon but has also been fighting in Syria for years. As noted, it has counterparts in Iraq and Yemen and many representatives in South America, all of which are under Iranian command. Iran has armed the Hezbollah with more than a hundred and thirty thousand rockets and hundreds of precision missiles in order to threaten Israel's home front. This is the firepower of a regular army. The Hezbollah serves as Iran's main card in Iran's threats against Israel. If the IDF attacks its nuclear facilities, the Hezbollah will act against its citizens and infrastructures. This is an attempt to form a balance of terror and deterrence.

A multi-barreled rocket launcher of the Hezbollah Organization carefully camouflaged in woodland in southern Lebanon and aimed at Israel. A major proportion of the Hezbollah's arms and the vast majority of its funding come from Iran.

Syria: The weak regime of President Assad, who has relied on religious and ethnic minorities – primarily Alawites and Shiites, needs Iran to survive the civil war. Iran has brought in thousands of Hezbollah fighters into Syria and employs tens of thousands of Shiite mercenaries. Most of these mercenaries are Shiite Afghan refugees who have fled to Iran. Under the combination of threats to their families (which may be expelled from Iran) and financial incentives (of barely 200-300 dollars a month), they are fighting the Sunni rebels in Syria in favor of Iranian interests. In Syria there are also thousands of Iranian "advisors" and the beleaguered country has become a staging point for arms convoys headed for the Hezbollah in Lebanon. Iran is building permanent bases in Syria of the Al Quds Force and is deploying long range missiles in it that are capable of threatening all of Israel, Jordan and other countries in the area. Since the spring of 2018, Israel has started to fight Iran more directly and overtly on Syrian soil. This is an attempt to prevent the consolidation of the Revolutionary Guards on Israel's northeastern border.

Rubble and destruction.A street in Raqqa, Syria, 2017.

In Yemen: In recent years there has been a war of attrition between Shiite (Houthi) rebels and the beleaguered regime. Saudi Arabia and the Gulf States are aiding the Yemeni (Sunni) regime and Iran on the other hand is investing great resources in assisting the Shiite rebels. Iranian missiles are launched from rebel territory at Saudi cities. These are ballistic missiles and some argue that this is a lethal test range of the Revolutionary Guards. In addition, rebels are deploying surface to sea missile batteries under Iranian auspices. They can currently hit any ship in the Red Sea passing Egypt next to Yemen. The Red Sea serves as an important sea lifeline to Saudi Arabia, Israel, Egypt and Jordan, all of which have important ports in it. Moreover, these missiles endanger any ship that attempts to pass through the strategic Suez Canal. In other words: Iran's proxy is capable of threatening to incapacitate one of the most important shipping lanes in the world.

Sudan: this large, poor and failed state is convenient ground for the Revolutionary Guards. Iran has logistic and organizational presence on Sudanese soil. Arms convoys have been sent from Sudan to everywhere that Iran has wanted. Some have been headed to the Gaza Strip and were bombed by unidentified aircraft, often claimed to be Israeli.

The Gaza Strip, the West Bank and Israel: the Gaza Strip has been controlled by more than a decade by the Hamas terrorist organization. Iran is a key patron of Palestinian terrorism that is threatening Israel from the direction of the Gaza Strip. Many of the rockets possessed by the Hamas and the Palestinian Islamic Jihad Organization were supplied by Iran. Iran paid Gazan "demonstrators" money to come to the border fence with Israel to cause violent provocations.

A number of terrorist cells and organizations enlisted by the Hezbollah have been uncovered and apprehended by Israel's security forces in recent years. Most of the organizations that have been neutralized originated from West Bank residents. Some of them consisted of Israeli Arabs. The Hezbollah does not operate this way without guidance from Iran, and it may therefore be said that Iran is also active within the State of Israel.

Bahrain: in 2011, masses from the oppressed Shiite majority in the small island of Bahrain went out to demonstrate against the Sunni royal family. The demonstrations occurred inter alia because of the encouragement of Iranian agents who promised support. The Sunni king asked for and got Saudi aid and a large Saudi military force landed in Bahrain, which along with the local police forces forcefully put an end to the protests. Nobody can promise that a protest will not break out again in the future or, that there will not be a Shiite rebellion on the island.

Morocco: the King of Morocco furiously ordered the severing of ties with Iran in early 2018. Despite the very great distance between Morocco and Iran, the Revolutionary Guards and the Hezbollah have supported the Polisario Front organization. This is a guerilla organization that is fighting Morocco over control of the western Sahara. The long arms of Iran have also reached the North African country on the Atlantic coast.

South America: there is extensive Iranian activity in many countries in South America, headed by Venezuela. Besides lawful commercial ties with Iran, there is also criminal activity to a scale of billions of dollars. Iran and the Lebanese Hezbollah are involved in drug trafficking, illegal trade of car parts, arms trading and money laundering, in cooperation with South American criminal organizations. This activity provides the Revolutionary Guards and the Hezbollah money while at the same time causing economic and moral damage and also costing lives in the countries in South America.

The President of Iran, Khatami, in a meeting with the President of Venezuela, Nicolas Maduro

Why is Iran operating
the way it is?

Iran's subversive activity is costing it a lot of money. In the Syrian Civil War alone, Iran is investing 6-15 billion dollars each year. Billions of dollars have been utilized for developing nuclear weapons, long range missiles and at the same time on running the various proxy organizations in many countries. The Iranian regime is paying a high price in its international visibility, is accumulating many enemies and is also looking very bad to many in the country itself. So it should be asked: why is it worth it? This question has no easy, clear answer. As always in international politics, the reasons are diverse and interwoven:

1. Economics – Iran is trying to achieve control, albeit indirectly, over areas that are rich in oil and natural gas. This applies primarily to Iraq, Bahrain and to a

lesser degree in Syria. The Iranian spread in the region will allow it to become a key exporter to economies of protégé countries. Iran will be able to become an even greater energy giant than today and to control trade routes on land, in the air and at sea. Such potential economic power will be able to help it contend with international sanctions in the future. At the same time it is important to remember Iran's massive cooperation with criminal organizations in South America, which also allows it to evade some of the sanctions.

2. Forming a "Shiite crescent" – on the world map – Iranian / Shiite dominance of the entire territory between Iran itself and the Mediterranean shores – through Iraq, Syria and Lebanon. These three countries contain a Shiite population and they will be subjected to the Islamic Republic. A modern revival of the ancient Persian Empire.

3. Export of the Islamic revolution to the Shiite world – Bahrain, Yemen, Syria, Afghanistan, Lebanon and Iraq. This is ideological thinking. After the spread of Iranian hegemony to the Shiite world, Iran will ensure protection of it and its values primarily against Sunni Muslims. Afterward it will be able to free up to continue to export the values of its Shiite Islamic revolution.

4. Land military reason – surrounding Iran's two greatest enemies in the Middle East, Israel and Saudi Arabia. Israel is surrounded by Iranian proxies on the Lebanese

border, Syrian border and in the Gaza Strip. Saudi Arabia is threatened from the directions of Iraq, Yemen and Bahrain.

5. Naval military reason – Iranian access to the Red Sea, the gateway to the Suez Canal, by taking over parts of Yemen and maintaining a presence in Sudan. Future Iranian presence on the Mediterranean shores may be able to come from Lebanon, the Gaza Strip and possibly in the future from Morocco too (which has an Atlantic coast). Bahrain is a strategic island in the Persian Gulf and there too, it must be recalled, Iran flexed its strength.

6. Like many regimes in the world, past and present, Iran is trying to divert the attention of its own people from severe economic problems instead of trying to solve them completely. A clash with and fight against external enemies, true and imagined, is an excellent way of achieving such misdirection.

Summary:

This article has provided a brief description of a number of characteristics of the Islamic Republic of Iran, with emphasis on its ambition of achieving nuclear weapons and regional dominance. The ayatollah regime is maintaining an aggressive foreign policy of expansion, while indirectly using force, by arming proxy organizations. In the last decade, the collapse of Arab countries has resulted in chaos around the Middle East and in North Africa. This has been an opportunity for Iran to advance its hegemony around the Middle East. We have been witnessing a serious Iranian attempt, involving an investment of considerable resources, to achieve power and status as a regional power and possibly even a global one. The Iranian emphasis is on areas with a Shiite population – Iraq, Syria, Bahrain, Lebanon and Yemen. However, there is also Iranian activity in areas in which Shia has no presence, such as in the Palestinian Territories, Morocco and Sudan.

Arab countries led by Saudi Arabia have not been able to form an effective coalition against Iran. Israel, despite its strong military capability, is limited in its ability to operate beyond its borders in order to stop Iran. There is currently no Middle Eastern player that is capable along of stopping Iran's spread. Therefore, only global powers can choose to stop Iran. However, China is not an adversary of Iran. Russia is managing a complex relationship with Iran consisting of interests (for example their joint support of the Assad regime in Syria). And what about European powers? They are not demonstrating, at the time of writing, any signs of strictness against Iran. Therefore, the Europeans appear to be interested primarily in trade with it, while cynically ignoring the bloody activity of the ayatollahs, which activity is responsible, alongside other reasons, for Muslim refugees and migrants to move to Europe.

In view of the foregoing, attention is being increasingly aimed at the world's "sheriff", the United States. The United States has been able to engender changes in Iranian policy in recent history by leading severe sanctions. This is owing to the urgent economic need of the Iranian regime to relieve the sanctions, which have almost led to a popular revolution. When coming to discuss the nuclear agreements with the global powers, the Iranians were in a position of absolute inferiority. However, despite, this, an agreement was signed in 2015, giving the Islamic Republic money, economic and political breathing space and international legitimacy, without demanding complete disbandment of its nuclear program or any mention of its subversive foreign activity. Therefore the project is continuing to develop at a partial level. This is in the form of development of ballistic missiles and retention of knowledge and equipment that is required for the day on which the country decides to reach beyond the completion of weapons. Once the agreement was signed, the Iranian regime started to increase its defense budget and redirected more and more resources to subversive foreign activity.

The United States' withdrawal from the nuclear agreement was a blow to the decision makers in Iran. The more moderate administration people in Iran, headed by President Rouhani, considered the agreement to be a major achievement. They hoped that the stalling, at least at the official level, of the nuclear plan, would relieve the economic stifling caused by the economic sanctions. However, the Iranian economy has not recovered as expected, certainly not when the conservatives in the Iranian regime, headed by its supreme leader Khamenei, are constantly increasing the defense budget. Today the United States is threatening not just to restore all the sanctions, but to intensify them too. The Europeans are facing a difficult dilemma. In the future they will have to choose between Iran and the United States, whose economy is 20 times that of the Islamic Republic.

In the near future, we can expect to see dramatic decisions of the various players in the region. We shall see how serious President Trump's United States is over the restoration and tightening of the sanctions. We shall see how the Europeans will respond, and most importantly, we shall soon see the counteraction of the Iranian regime. It may cover a spectrum of options: a defiant return to enrichment of uranium, increased subversive activity in the Middle East, an attempt to drive a wedge between Europe and the United States, flexibility and return to the negotiating table and more. There may be further changes in the future, but only the Iranian people can perform these, if it overcomes its fears. We are now entering another period of changes in the Middle East. All the pieces on the chessboard are waiting for players to move them.

Bibliography

ארליך. ח. (2017).*המזרח התיכון - המשבר הגדול ביותר מאז מוחמד*. ראשון לציון: ידיעות ספרים

בר זוהר. מ, משעל. נ. *המוסד - המבצעים הגדולים. ישראל. הוצאת ידיעות ספרים*.

הנדל. י, יעקב כץ, (2011). ישראל נגד איראן - מלחמת הצללים. אור יהודה: כנרת זמורה ביתן.

הרכבי. י. (1992). *מלחמה ואסטרטגיה*. תל אביב: משרד הביטחון.

מוריס. ב. (2003). *קורבנות: תולדות הסכסוך הציוני-ערבי 2001-1881*. תל אביב: ספריית אופקים.

נקדימון. ש. (2004). *תמוז בלהבות. ישראל: ידיעות אחרונות*.

סופר א. (2006). *המאבק על המים במזרח התיכון. תל אביב: עם עובד*.

Grinfeld A. (2017). *Echoes of war,* Israel/USA, Amazon press.

Haidar, J.I., (2015). Sanctions and Exports Deflection: Evidence from IranParis School of Economics, University of Paris

Lewis, B. (1993). *The Arabs in history.* England. Oxford university press.

Peres. S. (1993). *The new middle east.* Bnai-Brak: Stimatzki.

Razoux. P, *The iran-iraq war,* (2015), USA: Harvard

Scales H. Robert, *Certain victory,* (1993) Office of the chief of staff, US Army

Shavit. A. (2013). *My promised land.* New York:Shpiegel and Grau.

Articles:

Stecklow. S, Dehghanoisgeh. B, Torbati. Y. (2013), *Assets of the Ayatollah – The economic empire behind Iran's supreme leader.* Reuters investigates

Iran and Venezuela plan anti-U.S. fund, USA Today, 14 January 2007.

Asadzade, Peyman 19 October 2017. "Analysis - Iran's involvement in Syria is costly. Here's why most Iranians still support it". Retrieved 21 October 2017 – via www. WashingtonPost.com.

Koelbl, Susanne; Shafy, Samiha; Zand, Bernhard (9 May 2016). "Saudia Arabia Iran and the New Middle Eastern Cold War". Der Spiegel. Retrieved 17 June 2017.

About the writer:

Amit Grinfeld is a licensed tour guide in Israel, with 11 years of experience. He has a BA degree in history and international relations from the Hebrew University of Jerusalem and an MA degree in Public Policy from Tel Aviv University. Amit has guided hundreds of groups including youth, Birthright, family tours, Christian pilgrims, VIP visitors in Israel, official guests of the Ministry of Foreign Affairs, Donors of the JNF, Journalists, press, army and police units and more. Most recently Amit has been invited to lecture on his book "The Six Day War - 50 Years Later" throughout the United States. Amit is married and is a father of 3 young children. He serves in the IDF as a Staff Major in the home front command.